Voices *of* Freedom

Civil Rights in the United States and South Africa

Jackie Glasthal

Steck Vaughn™

A Harcourt Achieve Imprint

www.Steck-Vaughn.com
1-800-531-5015

Voices of Freedom: Civil Rights in the United States and South Africa
By Jackie Glasthal

Photo Acknowledgements
Cover ©Hiroji Kubota/Magnum Photos; t.o.c. ©Gene Herrick/AP Wide
World Photos; p. 5 ©Lynn Pelham/Time Life Pictures/ Getty Images;
p. 7 ©The Granger Collection, New York; p. 8 ©CORBIS; p. 10 ©Kean
Collection/Hulton Archive/Getty Images; p. 14 ©Gene Herrick/AP Wide
World Photos; p. 17 ©Bettman/CORBIS; p. 20 All rights reserved to Joe
Alper Photo Collection LLC. The photograph may not be reproduced
in any manner whatsoever without the written permission of the Joe
Alper Photo Collection LLC; p. 23 ©Bettman/CORBIS; p. 25 ©Hulton
Archive/Getty Images; p. 26 ©Bettman/CORBIS.

ISBN 1-4190-2289-X

Printed in the United States of America

2 3 4 5 6 7 8 152 12 11 10 09 08 07

Table of Contents

The Power of Song

Bishop Desmond Tutu, the South African leader, spent years fighting for the rights of blacks. In 1984, he stood outside a university building in Oslo, Norway. He was there to accept the Nobel Peace Prize.

Normally, the ceremony is held inside. A bomb threat forced everyone outdoors. The police searched for explosives, and Bishop Tutu started singing "We Shall Overcome." Everyone joined in.

That song has a long history. It's known as a "freedom song." The music came from Africa. African-Americans adapted the tune in the United States. They sang the song while they worked as slaves. It kept their spirits up. The song became popular again during the **civil** rights movement in the 1960s. Protestors sang it when they marched. It gave them hope.

That day in Oslo, Bishop Tutu sang the song as a reminder. He wanted the audience to recall the long struggle for civil rights around the world. The song was already a symbol of courage and progress. In response to the bomb threat, the song also reminded everyone that more work remained.

Marchers join Martin Luther King Jr. (second from right) in a chorus of "We Shall Overcome" in Montgomery, Alabama, in 1965.

CHAPTER ONE

Middle Passage

On the west coast of Africa, slave traders gathered. They lined up black men and women. The captives had chains on their ankles. They had lash marks on their backs. Soon, they were herded into ships. The horrible trip across the Atlantic was called the Middle Passage. Between 1500 and 1850, this brutal scene was repeated thousands of times.

These African men and women spoke different languages. They came from different tribes. They were Ashanti, Ibo, Wolof, Mandingo, and others. Yet they often had one thing in common: music. In most African cultures, music was a part of daily life. People sang while they worked. They sang to pass on their customs and beliefs. Some played drums to send messages from village to village.

Africans were packed onto slave ships more like cargo than people.

As they boarded the ships, the slaves had none of their belongings. They had nothing to remind them of home—except songs. So, they sang. One white observer **described** the scene on a ship in 1789. "I heard them singing, and then always tears. Their songs told the story of their grief."

At least 600,000 Africans were sold into slavery in North America. Most of them worked in the Southern states. They tended crops. They raised their masters' children. Laws kept slaves from learning to read and write. Husbands, wives, and children could be sold like cattle. Many family members never saw each other again.

In this life, music was **vital**. Slaves sang in the fields. They sang while they cooked. They sang at weddings and funerals and holidays. The music gave them comfort and strength.

Slave owners often misunderstood the singing. Some thought it showed that the slaves were happy with their lives. They often had black musicians play or sing at parties. Other owners had little **tolerance**

Slaves endured long days in the fields. Singing kept hope alive in difficult conditions.

for singing during work. Some planters allowed only lively songs in the fields. Slow songs, they thought, made the slaves work more slowly.

SINGING PRAYERS FOR FREEDOM

Many masters forced their slaves to go to church. The Africans didn't always appreciate the sermon, though. The preachers told them to obey their masters. The services were also quiet affairs. Hymns were sung softly. No one danced or showed much emotion. An African named Cornelius Garner complained, "We wanted to sing, pray, and serve God in our own way."

Many Africans did exactly that. Small groups of worshippers met in secret at night. They sang and prayed as they pleased. They matched the tunes they knew with lyrics from their masters' churches. The songs they invented are called spirituals.

For slaves, spirituals often had two meanings. They were about religious salvation. They were also about freedom. "Go Down Moses" is one of the best-known spirituals. It tells about a time when the Jews were slaves. They were captives of the pharaoh, or king, of Egypt. According to the Bible, Moses led the Jews to freedom. "*Go down, Moses,*" the song goes. "*Way down in Egypt land. / Tell ole Pharaoh, / Let my people go.*" To the African slaves, the song was about them, too.

Sometimes music could help slaves plan a **revolt**. Sunday morning, September 9, 1739, was one of those times. About 20 slaves escaped with guns they stole from their masters. They marched south along South Carolina's Stono River. To help spread the word, some beat "talking drums." Others shouted out "Liberty." More slaves joined the revolt. They killed several slave owners along the way.

By the end of the day, the Stono Rebellion was over. Many of the rebels died fighting. The revolt made slave owners nervous. Some Southern states outlawed drums and horns. A Georgia law banned all loud instruments.

The laws didn't stop slaves from escaping. Over the years, thousands of slaves fled to the free states of the North. Along the way, they stopped at secret hideouts. Their route was called the "Underground Railroad."

Slave owners used bloodhounds to track down escaped slaves. The spiritual "Wade in the Water" reminded fugitives to travel in streams or rivers. That way the dogs couldn't pick up their trail.

For slaves on the Underground Railroad, music carried hidden meanings. The song "Steal Away to Jesus" is one example. To slave owners, it sounded like a harmless hymn. Slaves, however, sang it to announce that they were ready to escape.

"Follow the Drinking Gourd" carried secret information, too. "The drinking gourd" was another name for the Big Dipper. Two stars in the Big Dipper's "bowl" point at the North Star. Escaping slaves followed the stars to make sure they were traveling north.

FREE AT LAST

In 1865, the Civil War ended slavery. Many freed slaves wanted to forget the spirituals. The songs brought back painful memories. Then, in 1871, some college students in Nashville, Tennessee, formed a singing group. They called themselves the Jubilee Singers.

The Jubilee Singers introduced the world to freedom songs. England's Queen Victoria welcomed the singing group. So did President Ulysses S. Grant.

Freedom songs influenced all kinds of music, including jazz, gospel, and blues. Those types of music inspired rock-and-roll and hip-hop. The power of freedom songs went beyond music, too. It even helped change unfair laws.

Slavery in America

1619 The first slaves in America arrive in Jamestown, Virginia.

1739 The Stono Rebellion takes place.

1740 Slave codes are passed banning "loud instruments."

1808 The United States bans the Atlantic slave trade.

1850 The Fugitive Slave Law is passed. It requires citizens in free states to help return runaway slaves.

1861 The Civil War begins.

1863 Abraham Lincoln signs the Emancipation Proclamation. The new law makes slavery illegal in the South.

1865 The Civil War ends. The 13th Amendment to the Constitution is passed. It abolishes slavery in the U.S.

CHAPTER TWO

"We Shall Overcome"

T he date was December 5, 1955. The place was Holt Street Baptist Church in Montgomery, Alabama. A group of ministers stood on the **pulpit**. Reverend Martin Luther King Jr. stood with them. At the time, he was only 26. A crowd of thousands filled the aisles of the church and poured out onto the street.

In the crowd was a soft-spoken woman. She was middle-aged, and she worked sewing clothes. Her name was Rosa Parks. Less than a week earlier, she had been arrested. What crime did this woman commit? She refused to give up her bus seat to a white person. In protest, Montgomery's black citizens started a **boycott**. They refused to ride the city buses.

The meeting at the church began. As it did, everyone joined together in song. The first hymn they sang was "Onward Christian Soldiers." Nearly 100 years before, it had inspired Union soldiers during the Civil War. Now it had a new meaning.

Reverend Martin Luther King Jr. addresses the crowd at the Holt Street Baptist Church on December 5, 1955, in Montgomery, Alabama.

A Long Way to Go

Slavery ended in 1865. Ninety years later, **equality** was still a long way off for African Americans. Many Southern states had passed "Jim Crow" laws. These laws kept blacks from voting. Schools, restaurants, hotels, and even water fountains were **segregated**. So were hospitals and parks. The laws said that "separate but equal" was fair. Almost always, the black facilities were **inferior**, not equal.

Starting with the Montgomery bus boycott, things began to change. Over the next ten years, black activists protested against **discrimination**. They held sit-ins, sitting together at the "whites only" lunch counters. They registered people to vote. They marched in the streets. Some whites joined them.

The protesters often sang. They sang at mass meetings. They sang on marches. They sang in jail. Many of the songs were the same freedom songs that slaves had sung 100 years earlier. These songs connected African Americans to their past struggles. They helped announce the civil rights message to the public. "The freedom songs are the soul of the movement," said Martin Luther King Jr.

Many civil rights activists learned freedom songs at Highlander Folk School in Mounteagle, Tennessee. Highlander taught about social **reform**. It **emphasized** nonviolent protest. In place of guns and fists, Highlander's activists used music.

Guy Carawan was the music director at Highlander. He taught freedom songs to his students. Soon, people started changing the words. One starts with, "Over my head, I see *trouble* in the air." Activist Bernice Johnson Reagon changed it to "*freedom* in the air." "Ain't Gonna Let Nobody Turn Me Around" was another popular song. Protesters took out the word "nobody." Instead, they sang the name of any person who tried to stop them.

In the streets and in schools, music brought people together. Total strangers felt united when they sang. In 1960, students started the sit-ins at segregated restaurants. In 18 months, 3,600 of them had been arrested. At a sit-in in Tennessee, police arrested nearly 80 people. One of them was a white activist named Candie Anderson.

In the Tennessee jail, blacks and whites were segregated. Candie sat in a cell with one other white woman. She could hear the others singing down the hall. Then they called down to her, "Hey, don't you know any songs?" Candie and her cellmate started singing with them. "It was a lifeline," she said.

For many activists, music was a source of courage, too. The Supreme Court had declared segregation illegal at bus stations. So, in the summer of 1961, a group of blacks and whites rode buses together through the South. The Freedom Riders wanted to make sure the Supreme Court decision was enforced. At stops, they often found angry whites waiting. Riders were sometimes yanked from their seats.

In May, the Freedom Riders pulled into Montgomery, Alabama. A mob greeted them with hammers, chains, and pipes. The riders braced themselves. They walked off of the bus. Many joined hands. They started singing "We Shall Overcome." Bernard Layfayette was one of them. "It was … a song of hope that we would survive," he said, "and that even if we in that group did not survive, then we as a people would overcome."

Some of the riders were seriously injured that day. All of them survived.

Freedom Riders such as these were often attacked. Angry mobs would throw rocks, slash tires, and even set buses on fire.

Americans saw the violence on TV. Many people were outraged. They began pressuring the government to end segregation.

In 1964, Congress responded. Lawmakers passed the Civil Rights Act. It outlawed segregation in public places. It also banned discrimination at jobs and schools. The next year, Congress passed the Voting Rights Act. This law protected blacks' right to vote.

Protesters had won legal equality. Yet, there was more to do. Many African Americans were still shut out of good jobs. Their children often went to poor schools with few resources.

In 1968, Martin Luther King Jr. was assassinated. That night, riots broke out across the country. A new "black power" movement had developed. It rejected the nonviolence of the civil rights activists. It also had its own kind of music—soul and funk. In 1968, singer James Brown had a top ten hit. It was called "Say It Loud, I'm Black and I'm Proud."

To many people, the old freedom songs were too meek. Still, Dr. King had known how powerful they could be. "We sing the freedom songs for the same reason the slaves sang them," he had said. "The songs add hope to our determination that 'We shall overcome, black and white together, we shall overcome someday'."

America's Civil Rights Movement

1955 Rosa Parks refuses to give her bus seat to a white man. She is arrested in Montgomery, Alabama.

1956 A 381-day bus boycott ends. Montgomery buses are finally desegregated.

1957 Federal troops help integrate schools in Little Rock, Arkansas. They escort nine African-American students to a white school.

1960 Sit-ins begin at segregated lunch counters in Greensboro, North Carolina.

1961 Freedom Rides begin throughout the South.

1963 Martin Luther King Jr. gives his "I Have a Dream" speech during the March on Washington.

1964 The Civil Rights Act of 1964 is passed. Race riots follow in New York City. Martin Luther King Jr. wins the Nobel Peace Prize.

1965 The Voting Rights Act is passed. Riots break out in the Watts section of Los Angeles.

1968 Martin Luther King Jr. is assassinated at his hotel in Memphis, Tennessee, at the age of 39. Riots break out in more than 100 U.S. cities.

Freedom Singer

In 1960, the Student Nonviolent Coordinating Committee (SNCC) was formed. Its first job was to organize sit-ins. One day, a group of members got together and started singing. That's when the SNCC Freedom Singers were born. Rutha Harris was a member of that group. Here are a few of her memories.

The original SNCC Freedom Singers traveled the country singing and raising awareness of civil rights issues. Rutha Harris is on the right.

What did you do as a Freedom Singer?

Our group was formed to raise funds for the SNCC and tell our story through song. We traveled around the country. We covered about 65,000 miles in nine months.

The songs we sang were taken from spirituals, gospel, and rhythm and blues. We would just change the lyrics to fit the occasion. There's a church song that goes "I woke up with my mind stayed on Jesus." In that particular song, we just changed "Jesus" to "freedom."

How did people respond when they heard you sing?

In most parts of the country, we got a really good response. When we traveled into Mississippi and Alabama, sometimes fear would come into me. Then, we just prayed and hoped for the best. It didn't turn us around. We kept going. Even when we were shot at, we would just get down at the bottom of our car and keep going.

The songs helped. Without them, there wouldn't have been a movement. They gave us hope, courage, and trust.

CHAPTER THREE

From Prisoner *to* President

B ishop Desmond Tutu grew up in South Africa. When he was young, he found a copy of an American magazine. In it, he read about Jackie Robinson. In 1947, Robinson became the first African American to play baseball in the major leagues. "Hey, man!" Tutu said to himself. "Here is a black man who has overcome all kinds of odds, and made it! I will make it, too."

African Americans launched their fight for civil rights in the 1950s. Tutu went on to lead black South Africans in their own freedom struggle. The odds against them were enormous.

Whites made up just 12 percent of the population in South Africa. Yet they had ruled the country for centuries. The Dutch were the first to arrive, in 1652. They made slaves of the native people. The British settled in South Africa in the early 1800s. They banned slavery. They tried to protect black Africans. But soon, the British settlers found gold and diamonds. Blacks were forced to work in the mines. It was hardly better than slavery. Conditions were poor. Wages were terrible.

SLEGS BLANKES.
EUROPEANS ONLY.

Like African Americans, blacks in South Africa were barred from "whites only" areas. In 1952, these South Africans protested against such segregation. They were all arrested for riding in this train car.

Descendants of the Dutch returned to power in 1910. They called themselves Afrikaners. In 1948, the unfair treatment of blacks became law. The system was called **apartheid**. In Afrikaans, the word means "apartness" or "separation." Under apartheid, blacks weren't allowed to vote. They couldn't own land. They couldn't marry whites. The government set up separate black areas called "homelands." To enter white areas, blacks had to carry special passes. Without a pass, they could be arrested.

Blacks resisted apartheid. They held strikes and peaceful marches. The African National Congress was formed to lead the movement. The government responded by arresting the movement's leaders. In 1964, they put ANC-leader Nelson Mandela in prison.

Step Lightly

In traditional South African culture, group music was a way of life. After the Dutch and British came, life changed. At mining camps, for instance, workers were banned from meeting in groups. Still, they gathered on weekends. Workers were far from their families. They were tired. Yet they were determined to sing.

Musicians formed teams and held contests. They took turns singing and dancing. Guards patrolled nearby, so the performers kept the noise low. The

South African activist Nelson Mandela (left) spent 26 years in prison for speaking out against apartheid.

music they played became known as *isicathamiya* (is-cot-a-ME-ya). The word is Zulu, South Africa's most widely-spoken language. It means to "step lightly" or "tip-toe."

Blacks all over South Africa had to "step lightly" in order to express themselves. The government closely watched books and movies. They didn't want writers or directors criticizing apartheid. The group in charge was called the Publications Control Board. The board often banned material about race relations.

The government also **censored** music. Security police recorded concerts. They decided which songs were "dangerous." Those songs were banned from the radio. Certain musicians were put on a **blacklist**. Blacklisted musicians weren't allowed to perform in public. Officers threatened club owners who hired blacklisted performers. One former officer admitted putting tear gas into a club's air conditioning system. Within moments, the club was empty.

Under apartheid, it became hard for musicians to make a living. Some groups performed on the street. They promoted their albums that way. The Mahotella

Queens sang outside record stores. Still, musicians could be jailed for singing "dangerous" songs.

Many musicians left the country. Miriam Makeba, Hugh Masekela, and Abdullah Ibrahim came to the United States. Ibrahim is a jazz pianist. He spent thirty years outside the country. "Many musicians died in **exile**," he says. "It was as though a generation had been totally wiped out."

Still, the music survived. One popular style is called kwela. It was first played in a black township called Soweto. In Zulu, *kwela* means "get up," or "climb on." It's a plea to start dancing. It's also the order police officers gave to people they arrested. The captives had to climb into a police van. In the townships, people called the vans "kwela-kwelas." Kwela music is often performed on pennywhistles. Kwela players often blew a warning when they saw a police van.

THE WORLD IS WATCHING

In the 1970s, protests rocked South Africa. And the world started to notice. In 1976, the government insisted that all schools in black homelands teach in Afrikaans instead of the native languages. Riots broke out that year in Soweto.

Police killed more than 500 protesters during the riots in Soweto in 1976. Students were protesting a ban on their native languages in schools.

On June 16, thousands of protesters filled the streets, singing as they marched. Police shot at them with tear gas and bullets. The rioters fought back. They pushed the police out of Soweto. Riots spread. The police returned with armored trucks. They killed more than 500 protesters, including children.

The world was outraged. Many countries stopped doing business with South Africa. Celebrities and musicians refused to perform there.

Finally, in 1990, President F. W. de Klerk released Nelson Mandela from prison. The government began to **repeal** the apartheid laws.

In 1994, free elections were held. On May 10, Mandela became South Africa's first black president. At his inauguration, Mandela reached out to both whites and blacks. He spoke partly in Afrikaans. He played two national anthems. One was an Afrikaner song. The other was "God Bless Africa." For years, the song had been banned by the government. Now, it was a national anthem.

When the band finished playing, someone shouted out "*amandla*." That means "power." The crowd shouted back "*awethu*." It means "to the people." After that, someone began singing, "We Shall Overcome." The whole crowd, black and white, joined in. Under President Nelson Mandela, **justice** finally came to all the South African people.

South Africa's Liberation Movement

1652 The Dutch settle in present-day South Africa.

1795 The British seize Capetown from the Dutch.

1867 Diamonds are discovered in southern Africa.

1886 Gold is discovered in southern Africa.

1910 South Africa becomes an independent nation.

1913 The Native Lands Act limits land ownership by blacks.

1948 Apartheid officially becomes the law of the land.

1951 Black Africans are relocated into segregated "homelands."

1952 Nelson Mandela organizes nonviolent resistance throughout South Africa.

1964 Nelson Mandela is sentenced to life in prison.

1976 Hundreds are killed during the Soweto uprising.

1990 Mandela is freed. Apartheid officially ends.

1994 Mandela is elected president.

Glossary

apartheid *(noun)* a South African political policy that kept different races apart

blacklist *(noun)* a list of people who have been banned from doing something

boycott *(noun)* the refusal to buy or take part in something as a way of protesting

censor *(verb)* to remove parts from books, movies, music, etc., thought to be harmful

civil *(adjective)* having to do with the people of a country, not its military or religion

descendants *(noun)* your descendants are your children, their children, and so on

describe *(verb)* to tell or write about something

discrimination *(noun)* prejudiced treatment or action against someone or something by others

emphasize *(verb)* to highlight or make a point about something

equality *(noun)* fair or equal treatment for everyone

exile *(noun)* the condition of not being allowed into one's own country

inferior *(adjective)* not as good as something or someone else

justice *(noun)* the upholding of equal rights for all persons under the law

pulpit *(noun)* a raised platform where a minister stands

reform *(noun)* a change for the better; an improvement

repeal *(verb)* to cancel or undo something

revolt *(noun)* a rebellion against someone in power

segregate *(verb)* to separate people or groups of people

tolerance *(noun)* the willingness to put up with something

vital *(adjective)* very important

IDIOMS

mind stayed on *(page 21)* to think about one thing constantly
During the test, my mind stayed on the subject.

Index